Whispers
of the Inner-Mind

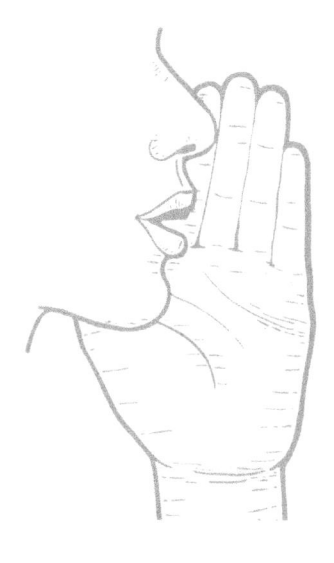

Echoes of the Soul for Enhancing Mindful Awareness,

Emotional Resilience and Inner Awakening

SWAMINATHAN MURALI

TABLE OF CONTENTS

Foreword.......*04*

Prologue.......*09*

   01. *"Rainbow In The Rain"* *13*

   02. *"Dancing With Dinos"* *15*

   03. *"Together We Stand"* *18*

   04. *"Lifted Fears"*.......*21*

   05. *"Dancing With The Unknown"* *23*

   06. *"The Gentle Flame Of Inspiration"* *25*

   07. *"Emotional Alchemy"* *27*

   08. *"Nunchi"* *31*

   09. *"The Orchard Of Generosity"* *34*

   010. *"Echoes Of Lost Heritage"* *37*

   011. *"Embracing Peace Through Acceptance"* *40*

   012. *"The Full Moon"* *43*

   013. *"The Ocean 'S Lament"* *46*

   014. *"Whispers Of Dawn"* *49*

   015. *"Speculative Thinking"* *52*

016. "Pedaling Beyond Comfort" …….54

017. "Beyond The Comfort Zone" …….56

018. "Mirrors Of Positivity And Growth" ……. 59

019. "Switching Perceptive" …….61

020. "The Weight Of Thoughts"…….64

021. "Echoes Of Identity"…….67

022. "Embracing Optimism" …….70

023. "Faith" …….72

024. "Disturbed Dream" …….74

025. "Realms Of Astral Planes" …….76

Epilouge…….78

About The Author…….81

Your Valuable Review…….82

Other Books From The Author…….83

Acknowledgement…….88

Copyright…….89

FOREWORD

In Whispers of the Inner Mind, each poem beckons readers into the soul's quiet, often overlooked corridors, offering gentle reflections on inner growth, resilience, and the extraordinary facets of human experience.

This collection, meticulously crafted as "Echoes of the Soul for Enhancing Mindful Awareness, Emotional Resilience, and Inner Awakening," resonates with the universal desire for connection, introspection, and understanding. Within these pages, the words do more than convey; they invite a dance with the self, sparking introspection and encouraging readers to embark on a journey where the heart and mind engage in mutual dialogue.

The introductory poem, **"Rainbow in the Rain,"** establishes this theme of embracing life's dualities. The reader is reminded through vivid imagery and gentle rhythm that beauty often emerges in adversity.

This piece symbolises the resilience and hope that each of us carries, even amid life's inevitable storms.

In **"Dancing with Dinos,"** nostalgia blends with playfulness, sparking a lighthearted journey back to innocence. The poem reminds us of the importance of imagination and our capacity to find wonder in life, urging readers to rekindle the lost spark of childhood curiosity.

"Together We Stand" highlights unity and shared humanity, underscoring the value of standing together amidst challenges. Its simplicity and strength embody the message of collective resilience, a theme further expanded upon in **"Lifted Fears,"** where courage and support help transcend personal limitations. Through evocative verses, these poems remind us that we are stronger when we uplift each other.

The collection transitions gracefully to **"Dancing with the Unknown,"** a tribute to embracing life's uncertainties. The reader is encouraged to step forward with faith, even without a clear path. This sentiment is further echoed in **"The Gentle Flame of Inspiration,"** a piece that ignites motivation, inviting readers to connect with their inner source of light.

Each title reveals a unique layer of the human experience. **"Emotional Alchemy"** guides us through transforming our inner struggles into wisdom, reminding us that resilience is built through self-reflection and acceptance. Similarly, **"Nunchi"** introduces readers to the Korean concept of empathy and situational awareness, skillfully blending cultural wisdom with a universal call for mindfulness in our interactions.

In **"The Orchard of Generosity,"** kindness and abundance blossom, reflecting the idea that when we give selflessly, we cultivate growth not only in ourselves but also in those around us. This theme finds a quiet counterpart in **"Echoes of Lost Heritage,"** a nostalgic ode honouring past generations and urges us to remember and cherish the roots that have shaped our identity.

"Embracing Peace Through Acceptance" and **"The Full Moon"** guide readers to find serenity by aligning with the natural rhythms of life. Here, peace is not sought through control but through surrender to life's ebb and flow, beautifully illustrated by the moon's cyclical journey.

In **"The Ocean's Lament,"** we hear a soulful plea from nature, a reminder of our interconnection with the world and our responsibility to protect it. **"Whispers of Dawn"** provides a contrast, representing the quiet moments of reflection that dawn brings, suggesting that each day is a fresh opportunity to listen to the whispers within.

"Speculative Thinking" and *"Pedaling Beyond Comfort"* invite readers to expand their mental horizons, encouraging a mindset that thrives beyond self-imposed limits. This theme of growth beyond comfort zones recurs in *"Beyond the Comfort Zone,"* where the author dares readers to stretch their boundaries and redefine personal limitations.

As the collection progresses, *"Mirrors of Positivity and Growth"* and *"Switching Perspective"* delve into the power of perspective. Shifting our view reminds us that positivity and growth often wait on the other side of our assumptions. *"The Weight of Thoughts"* similarly addresses the impact of mindset, illustrating how thoughts can either weigh us down or uplift us, depending on how we choose to carry them.

"Echoes of Identity" asks readers to reflect on the multifaceted nature of the self, exploring how personal identity is defined by and distinct from our roles, relationships, and experiences. This exploration is met with hope in *"Embracing Optimism,"* a poem that radiates encouragement, urging readers to cultivate a mindset of possibility.

In **"Faith,"** we encounter a deep sense of spiritual resilience. Faith here is not limited to religion but is a broader sense of trust in life's unfolding. **"Disturbed Dream"** contrasts this, reflecting on the challenges that disrupt our inner peace and the resilience we build in the process. The poem mirrors the discomfort we often feel and the wisdom from these uncomfortable awakenings.

Finally, **"Realms of Astral Planes"** provides a transcendent close to the collection. This poem dives into metaphysical realms, inviting readers to explore mysteries beyond the material world. Here, the journey through the "inner mind" reaches a profound crescendo as we are reminded that our inner landscape is vast, boundless, and endlessly worth exploring.

Whispers of the Inner Mind is a profound reminder that poetry is more than mere words; it is an invitation to listen to the unspoken, to feel beyond the tangible, and to trust in the transformative power of inner reflection. Each poem calls to embrace every part of oneself—the familiar and the foreign, the light and the shadow. It is this wholeness that brings forth true inner harmony.

PROLOGUE

Whispers of the Inner Mind opens as an invitation—a gentle call to the reader to embark on an intimate journey within. In a world that moves with relentless speed, where moments of quiet introspection have become rare luxuries, this collection is a pause, a breath, a mirror held up to the self. Within these pages, each poem serves as a gateway, leading to hidden chambers within the mind and heart that often go unexplored in the hustle of daily life.

In an era of information overload and constant connectivity, silence has grown rare, and with it, so has the ability to listen—not only to the world around us but also to the quiet, persistent whispers within.

These are the whispers of intuition, unresolved questions, joy and sorrow, each waiting for a moment of acknowledgement. This collection dares to quiet the noise, to pull back the veil, and to take readers through a journey of introspection that is both gentle and profound. As you read, you may find echoes of your own experiences, feelings, and thoughts mirrored in the verses reminders of shared humanity and the universal language of the soul.

The journey begins with "Rainbow in the Rain," an ode to resilience and beauty found even in life's most challenging moments. This theme is not a call to gloss over pain but a reminder of our quiet strength. Like this one, each poem affirms that life's struggles can be transformed into more profound wisdom through the alchemy of introspection. The poems beckon you to explore each experience, thought, and feeling as a vital piece of the mosaic that forms the self. In this exploration, you may find healing, transformation, and a renewed self-compassion.

As the reader progresses, each title hints at an aspect of life we often overlook or avoid—perhaps because it feels too tender, unsettling, or unknown. But here, you are encouraged to walk through these spaces without fear. "Dancing with Dinos" reminds us of the simplicity and joy of imagination, inviting the reader back to a time when curiosity and wonder defined each moment. "Together We Stand" and "Lifted Fears" speak to the power of connection, of shared experiences that allow us to lean on one another, revealing a deep sense of unity that transcends words.

In the spirit of mindfulness, these poems are crafted to linger and leave an impression long after being read. Each one is a seed, planted in the fertile ground of the reader's awareness, inviting contemplation that goes beyond the written word. The verses do not seek to provide definitive answers; instead, they open doors to new questions, encouraging readers to ponder their interpretations and responses.

This book is, at its core, an exploration of emotional alchemy—the practice of transforming the raw materials of experience into insight, compassion, and acceptance. Through poems like "Emotional Alchemy," "The Gentle Flame of Inspiration," and "The Orchard of Generosity," the reader is guided through processes of inner transformation. These are not lofty, abstract ideas but simple truths grounded in our shared lived experiences. They are invitations to engage with one's inner world, honour the full spectrum of emotions and experiences that define us, and emerge with a more profound sense of self-awareness and purpose.

As you embark on this journey, allow yourself to feel, imagine, and reflect without judgment. This collection does not demand a linear reading or structured interpretation.

Each poem stands on its own yet weaves into the larger tapestry of themes that speak to resilience, transformation, and the gentle unfolding of the self.

In this prologue, I invite you to let each poem be a touchstone, a guide, and a quiet companion on your journey through the inner landscape of your mind. May the whispers you encounter in these pages inspire comfort and awaken a deeper connection with the vast, mysterious, and beautiful terrain within.

01

"RAINBOW IN THE RAIN"

Beneath the silver sky, they walk in line,

A symphony of hues, a vibrant sign.

Each step they take, a dance upon the street,

With raindrops playing melodies so sweet.

Umbrellas bloom like flowers in the grey,

A rainbow in the mist, they light the way.

In every stride, a whisper of delight,

As colours blend and shimmer in the night.

©Swaminathan Murali

02

"DANCING WITH DINOS"

"Tiny Dancer, Colorful Roar"

With crayons bright, and a heart full of cheer,

A tiny artist brought a dinosaur near.

With colours bold, and a stroke of delight,

He brought to life a prehistoric sight.

As the final stroke hit the paper with flair,

He jumped up high without a single care.

His feet began to move with a happy grace,

A dance of joy, a smile on his face.

His roars of laughter echoed through the air,

As he twirled and spun, without a single care.

His dinosaur came to life, it seemed to say,

"Let's celebrate colourfully!"

In this moment, pure joy did abound,

A carefree heart, a spirit unbound.

May his creativity and joy always shine,

And his love for life will forever be divine.

©Swaminathan Murali

The sheer bliss of my 3-year-old grandson colouring dinos

It's a celebration of the joy and creativity of childhood and the special moments that make life so precious.

"TOGETHER WE STAND"

Love one another, yet give each other space,

For the oak and the cypress grow not in each other's embrace.

Let the winds of heaven dance between your souls,

For in that freedom, true unity unfolds.

Sing and dance together, in joy and in sorrow,

Yet remember, each soul must find its own tomorrow.

Drink from the same cup, yet not the same drink,

For even in oneness, let your individuality think.

Stand close together, yet not too near,

For the pillars of the temple stand apart, clear.

The strings of a lute, though separate they are,

In harmony, they create a melody from afar.

Ubuntu, we live, in each other's light,

For I am because we are, shining bright.

Your joy is mine, your sorrow my pain,

Together, we rise, again and again.

Build bridges of compassion, walls of trust,

In this human family, kindness is a must.

Share your bread, but let your hearts be free,

For in giving, we find our true identity.

Let your love be like the river, flowing wide and free,

Nurturing all it touches to be the best they can be.

Love one another, not to possess or bind,

But to lift each other, body, soul, and mind.

©Swaminathan Murali

This scribble is based on reading Khalil Gibran's poem

LOVE ONE ANOTHER

and I have included the famous principle of UBUNTU, which originated in South Africa. I AM BECAUSE WE ARE.

An English teacher in South Africa guiding a group of about fifty underprivileged children offered a bag of chocolates to a child who came first after touching a tree fifty meters apart in a race. All the children ran, hugged the tree, and came back together, shouting UBUNTU in their native language. Thus, the anecdote of the famous principal of UBUNTU goes on as they share the chocolates.

04

"LIFTED FEARS"

In enclosed spaces, I feel confined.

My heart races fast, my soul entwined

With every floor, my anxiety grows

A sense of trap; my freedom it knows

The doors slide shut, a claustrophobic night

My breath is short; my pulse takes flight

I'm trapped and helpless, my mind a mess

A prisoner of fear in this metal nest

The lift ascends, and my fears intensify.

A sense of doom, my heart can't deny

But still, I ride through the painful test

And hope that calm will eventually find rest

©Swaminathan Murali

Note: The phobia of moving in lifts is known as Liftophobia or Elevatophobia. This poem aims to capture the feelings associated with this phobia and is not meant to be a professional representation or solution. It is based on my real-life experience of being taped alone in an 11-story building for about three hours until help rushed in.

05

"DANCING WITH THE UNKNOWN"

In the dance of life, so wild and free,

Where certainty's a fleeting dream,

We learn to sail the uncharted sea,

To trust the stars, to let things be.

With every wave that rocks our boat,

With every storm we brave and fight,

We find the strength to stay afloat,

And greet the dawn with newfound light.

For in the heart of the unknown,

Lie wonders waiting to unfold,

In each uncertainty, we've grown,

And found our courage, strong and bold.

So let us dance with open hearts,

Embrace the twists, the twirls, the flow,

For in this dance, each step imparts,

A joy that only we can know.

©Swaminathan Murali

06

"THE GENTLE FLAME OF INSPIRATION"

In the heart of dreams, where ideas bloom,

A gentle flame can light the room.

Not with force or pushy might,

But with a glow so warm and bright.

Passion whispers, softly calls,

Breaking through the rigid walls.

Enthusiasm, pure and true,

Spreads a light that all pursue.

Like Leonardo with his art,

He shared his vision, heart to heart.

No need to push, no need to shove,

He drew them in with earnest love.

So let your dreams take gentle flight,

Inspire others with your light.

For in the warmth of shared delight,

Ideas will soar to wondrous heights.

©Swaminathan Murali

"EMOTIONAL ALCHEMY"

In the crucible of my heart's forge,

Emotions blend like metals rare,

From leaden depths to golden soar,

Transformed by alchemy's ancient flair.

Fear, the heavy, burdensome weight,

Melts with courage's steadfast flame,

In the heat of trials and fate,

Strength emerges, forged by pain.

Sadness, a tear-stained veil of gray,

Dissolves with joy's effervescent light,

In laughter's dance and love's array,

Hope blossoms from the darkest night.

Anger, fiery tempest of the soul,

Tempered by patience's gentle flow,

In forgiveness' embrace made whole,

Peace finds its haven, calm aglow.

Through trials and tests, emotions blend,
Alchemy of heart, mind, and soul,
Where shadows fade, and truths transcend,
In the alchemy that makes us whole.

Thus, in the crucible's sacred art,
I find the essence of my being,
Transformed by wisdom, forged by heart,
Emotional alchemy, life's truest freeing.

In every tear, a diamond's gleam,
In every fear, a warrior's dream,
In every pain, a healing balm,
In every storm, a peaceful calm.

Emotions, raw and unrefined,
Through alchemy's touch, they are refined,

Into the gold of wisdom's light,

Emotional alchemy, burning bright.

In this journey of heart's alchemy,

I find my truth, my deepest plea,

To understand, to heal, to grow,

In emotions' dance, life's ebb and flow.

Emotional alchemy, sublime art,

Where heart and soul find their restart,

In every feeling, every hue,

Alchemy transforms, and I renew.

©Swaminathan Murali

I scribbled this to get ideas for my forthcoming book on the same title.

08

"NUNCHI"

In life's intricate dance, there's a subtle art,

A skill that sets the wise and keen apart.

With eyes that see beyond mere words and glance,

Comes forth the mastery of Nunchi's trance.

Not bound by spoken tales or gestures grand,

But attuned to the unspoken, silent land.

In every room, a symphony it plays,

A harmony of cues in subtle ways.

With Nunchi's grace, one navigates the stream,

Reading hearts, unraveling the unseen.

In a glance, the depths of truth unfold,

In a whisper, secrets ancient and untold.

It's the gentle touch of empathy's hand,

The art of knowing when to make a stand.

In silence, understanding finds its voice,

In stillness, hearts connect and souls rejoice.

So, let us hone this art with tender care,

For Nunchi's wisdom is beyond compare.

In every moment, let our senses soar,

And grasp the truths that lie at wisdom's core.

©Swaminathan Murali

I was reading about NUNCHI as Emotional Intelligence is my bailiwik.

A brief from Google about NUNCHI

Nunchi, sometimes noonchi (눈치), is a Korean concept signifying the subtle art and ability to listen and gauge others' moods. It first appears in the 17th century as nunch'ŭi (眼勢 in hanja), meaning "eye force/power". In Western culture, nunchi could be described as the concept of emotional intelligence

.

09

"THE ORCHARD OF GENEROSITY"

In the orchard of generosity, where kindness blooms,

Amidst the whispering leaves and fragrant perfumes,

Stands a gardener, humble and wise,

Whose heart is a sanctuary, where compassion lies.

Beneath the boughs of an ancient tree,

He welcomes all, both humble and free,

With hands outstretched, he offers a gift,

A bounty of love, a spirit uplifted.

For in the act of giving, his soul finds release,

And the burdens of life seem to find their peace.

No drought can wither his spirit's grace,

For abundance resides in his warm embrace.

Like the cycle of seasons, his generosity flows,

A symphony of abundance, a melody that glows,

For what he bestows upon the weary heart,

Returns to him, a gift of art.

So let us learn from this gardener's creed,

That in giving, we find all that we need,

For in the orchard of generosity's bloom,

We discover the richness that dispels all gloom.

©Swaminathan Murali

010

"ECHOES OF LOST HERITAGE"

In the hush of time, our culture now a dream,

Ancient echoes silenced, a silent scream.

Temples whisper tales in crumbling stone,

Lost scriptures in dust, secrets once known.

Sanskrit hymns, a fading cosmic dance,

Echoes of Rasa, lost in a trance.

Bharatanatyam, a story untold,

Culture's heritage, now grown cold.

Traditions adorned in vibrant hues,

Veiled in modernity, obscured views.

Bindis and bangles, symbols so pure,

Lost in transition, traditions endure.

Mehendi patterns, intricate and wise,

Tales of ancestors in ancient skies.

Lost echoes linger, yearning for revival,

In the fabric of time, a cultural survival.

Yet, in the shadows, a resilience gleams,

As dreams of heritage break through the seams.

A journey to reclaim what time has stolen,

Our lost culture, a story yet unbroken.

©Swaminathan Murali

011

"EMBRACING PEACE THROUGH ACCEPTANCE"

In the calm of twilight's gentle embrace,

Where shadows dance and time finds its grace,

A lamp once cherished, now lies in shards,

A lesson unfolds, beyond mere regards.

"I would have preferred," the wise man said,

"That this lamp stayed whole, its light not shed.

Yet now that it's broken, I find my way,

To peace and calm at the end of the day."

For in life's dance, where moments twist,

Not every wish can persist.

The rain may fall where sun was sought,

And rudeness where kindness ought.

"I would prefer if people were kind,

But when they're not, peace I still find.

For it's not their actions that shape my day,

But how I choose to feel, come what may."

So let the storm and the sunshine play,

In the tapestry of each passing day.

With preferences gentle, expectations light,

We find our peace, our inner light.

Embrace the now, with open heart,

From life's designs, do not depart.

For in acceptance, true wisdom lies,

A tranquil mind, beneath vast skies.

©Swaminathan Murali

This poem reflects the philosophy of embracing peace through acceptance, focusing on the power of adjusting our expectations and finding calm within, regardless of external circumstances

.

012

"THE FULL MOON"

The full moon rises high,

Illuminating the sky,

With its soft silver light,

Bringing calmness to sight.

Casting its spell on earth,

With its alluring, mystical mirth,

Inspiring love and mystery,

Bringing peace and serenity.

So let's bask in its bright hue,

And enjoy the full moon's view,

For it is a symbol of power,

With lot of love in this hour.

Under the silver glow of the moon,

The night comes alive, so serene and boon.

Its light shines bright and bathes the earth,

Bringing peace and calm to all its girth.

The full moon rises, big and round,
Its radiance spreads all around.
With its beauty, it lifts the heart,
And its light never seems to depart.

On this night, the sky shines so bright,
With stars twinkling, a celestial sight.
And with the gentle Zephyr
Its light makes everything feel lighter.

So let us bask in the moon's light,
And adsorb its ethereal sight.
For it's a reminder of the power of nature,
And the peace that it brings, now and forever.

©Swaminathan Murali
I scribbled on enjoying the full moon with my grandson on the terrace.

013

"THE OCEAN 's LAMENT"

I weep for the depths that once were mine

Now filled with plastic, a toxic shrine

My waves that once crashed with majestic might

Now carry the weight of humanity's blight

My creatures that swam with grace and poise

Now struggle to survive in a world of noise

My coral reefs that bloomed with vibrant hue

Now bleach and wither, a sight anew

I mourn the loss of my pristine shore

Now littered with waste, forever more

My waters that once sang a soothing song

Now groan with the burden of what's been done wrong

Yet still I hold hope in my darkest night

For a chance to heal, a chance to ignite

A spark of change in the human heart

To restore my beauty, to set me apart.

©*Swaminathan Murali*

This poem is a reflection of the ocean's suffering due to human activities, such as pollution, overfishing, and climate change. The ocean's lament is a call to action, urging us to make a change and restore its former glory.

014

"WHISPERS OF DAWN"

In the hush before the morning light,

Where dreams and daybreak softly meet,

The world awakens from the night,

In silence, secrets bittersweet.

A golden ray, a tender kiss,

The darkness fades, the shadows cease,

The world is bathed in tranquil bliss,

In dawn's embrace, a silent peace.

The whispers of the morning breeze,

A symphony of nature's grace,

The rustling leaves, the song of trees,

In dawn's light, we find our place.

With every breath, a new beginning,

The fleeting moments gently flow,

In stillness, we find the meaning,

In dawn's glow, our spirits grow.

Embrace the dawn, the light within,

A journey to the soul's deep core,

In silence, let the day begin,

In dawn's light, we become more.

©Swaminathan Murali

"SPECULATIVE THINKING"

In the realm of thought's vast sea,
Where what could be meets what might be,
Ideas dance on fragile wings,
A world of endless wonder springs.

What ifs and maybes intertwine,
In the corridors of the mind,
Possibilities unfold,
In whispers of the yet untold.

With every thought, a thread is spun,
In speculative webs begun,
A future sketched in shades of gray,
In dreams that guide us through the day.

© Swaminathan Murali

016

"PEDALING BEYOND COMFORT"

Wheels once steady, now set free,

A trembling start, a heart's decree.

Fear and thrill, hand in hand,

Wobbling steps, a new command.

From comfort's clasp, we break away,

Into the sun, where boldness plays.

Each pedal stroke, a daring leap,

Into the vast, the unknown deep.

Stagnant paths behind us lie,

As we embrace the open sky.

With trust and courage, we ascend,

To places where our spirits mend.

Life's a ride, an endless flight,

A journey from the dark to light.

So pedal forth, and don't look back,

Adventure calls, on freedom's track.

©Swaminathan Murali
I scribbled on seeing my grandson learning to control his cycle.

017

"BEYOND THE COMFORT ZONE"

In shadows deep where fears reside,

Lies a path yet unexplored,

Where dreams and courage coincide,

A journey to the soul's core.

Beyond the walls of safe and known,

Where comfort keeps its reign,

There's a place where seeds are sown,

In fields of joy and pain.

Life whispers softly, "Come and see,

The wonders that await,

For within you lies the key,

To unlock your destined fate."

With every step in lands untamed,

The heart begins to grow,

And though the world may seem unchanged,

Inside, the rivers flow.

So trust the path, though dark and wide,

With courage as your guide,

For life provides and walks beside,

In whom we must confide.

Beyond the comfort, we are free,

To spread our wings and fly,

To embrace the vast infinity,

And reach beyond the sky.

©Swaminathan Murali

018

"MIRRORS OF POSITIVITY AND GROWTH"

In mirrors, reflections of the soul's gaze,
A sonnet weaves of clarity's embrace.
Thoughts crystallize in clarity's haze,
Transparent hearts, emotion's tender grace.

Still presence, like a mirror on the wall,
Reflects the best within, a polished gleam.
In introspection's light, we stand tall,
A mirror for the world, a tranquil stream.

Seeds planted, positive and profound,
In fertile soil of time, they gently grow.
Tomorrow's harvest, in today, is found,
A sonnet of resilience, let it show.

Dear friends, be mirrors to the hearts you see,
In clarity and stillness, let love be.

©Swaminathan Murali

"SWITCHING PERCEPTIVE"

In realms of thought, perceptions dwell,

A dance of minds, where stories swell,

With every step, perspectives shift,

In labyrinthine paths adrift.

From varied lenses, worlds arise,

A kaleidoscope before our eyes,

Through shifting prisms, colors blend,

New vistas found, old ones transcend.

The sun may rise, the moon may wane,

Yet in this dance, no truth is plain,

For as we twist and turn our view,

Our hearts unlock a broader hue.

With open minds and hearts aware,

We shed old skins, release the snare,

In every twist, we find our grace,

And see the world with fresh embrace.

In switching realms of light and shade,

New wisdoms bloom, foundations laid,

So let us cherish this grand art,

To switch perceptions, soulful start.

©Swaminathan Murali

020

"THE WEIGHT OF THOUGHTS"

In the quiet of my mind's embrace,

A storm of thoughts begins to trace,

A path of shadows, dark and deep,

Where restless spirits never sleep.

The world outside, a mirror plain,

Reflects within, an echo's strain,

And in this dance of night and day,

I find myself led far astray.

Blame the world, I often do,

For all the woes that I construe,

Yet in the stillness, truth reveals,

The source of all my inner ills.

The thoughts I hold, a burdensome weight,

Twist my fate, instigate,

A punishment of my own design,

In tangled webs of the mind's confine.

But what if I could let them go,

Like leaves upon a river's flow? T

o free my heart from their demand,

And find the strength to gently stand.

For in the act of setting free,

The chains that bind eternally,

I liberate my soul's own flight,

Into the realms of peace and light.

So here I vow, with steadfast heart,

To from these shadows swift depart,

To breathe, to live, to softly tread,

Beyond the echoes in my head.

©Swaminathan Murali

"ECHOES OF IDENTITY"

In the mirror's silent gaze, I seek,

A reflection of the self I peek.

A puzzle of hues, a canvas of light,

In shadows and whispers, I take flight.

Nature's brush and nurture's hand,

Crafting the essence, where I stand.

Threads of ancestry, woven deep,

In the depth of dreams, I sleep.

From the cradle's soft embrace,

To the world's vast, unfathomable space,

I journey forth, a wandering soul,

Seeking answers, to make me whole.

In the dance of culture, I find my part,

A symphony of voices, a beat of heart.

Yet beneath the masks, the roles we play,

Lies a truth that yearns to say:

"I am more than what you see,

A kaleidoscope of possibility.

In the labyrinth of thought, I roam,

Claiming my essence, finding home."

So let us embrace the quirks we bear,

The scars, the laughter, the silent prayer.

For in the mystery of "Why am I like this?",

Lies the poetry of our existence's kiss.

©Swaminathan Murali

I was contemplating the topic for my next book, WHY AM I LIKE THIS, and scribbled this one.

022

"EMBRACING OPTIMISM"

In the countdown of time, we weave,

Our past and present, they interleave.

Each moment a thread, each choice a line,

In the grand design of life's design.

Though storms may rage and darkness fall,

Within us burns a light, through all.

Optimism, like a beacon bright,

Guides us through the darkest night.

With courage firm and spirits high,

We face the challenges, we reach the sky.

For in our hands, the power lies,

To shape our fate beneath the skies.

So let us greet each dawn anew,

With hope and faith, our hearts imbue.

For in optimism's gentle sway,

We find the strength to seize the day.

©Swaminathan Murali

"FAITH"

In faith's embrace, we find our guiding light,

A beacon in the darkness, shining bright.

With every step, we trust the path unknown,

For faith instills the courage to be shown.

Through trials faced with steadfast certainty,

We rise above, fueled by divinity.

No need for every detail to be clear,

For faith assures the outcome we hold dear.

Like passengers aboard a plane in flight,

We soar on wings of trust, beyond our sight.

In faith, we find the strength to persevere,

To conquer doubts and quench our every fear.

So let us live with faith, in heart and soul,

And find in its embrace our truest goal.

©Swaminathan Murali

"DISTURBED DREAM"

The wavering mind

Wandering like the wind

So swift and random

Bringing Quality new ideas

Winking new thoughts

Pondering new ideas

Is it the Eureka moment

Or the apple fall

Tringg goes the alarm

With random eye movement

Half asleep snoozing the clock

Oh! It was a dream at last.

©Swaminathan Murali

025

"REALMS OF ASTRAL PLANES"

In realms astral, beyond earthly bounds,

Where consciousness roams in mystical rounds.

Hidden dimensions secrets unfold,

Cosmic wisdom whispers, stories untold.

Journeying far, through time and space,

Awakening souls in the divine embrace.

Exploring the depths, where dreams take flight,

In realms astral, where all is light.

In astral realms, where spirits dance,

Eternal echoes in cosmic expanse.

Embracing the journey with hearts aglow,

In realms of wonder, we endlessly grow.

©Swaminathan Murali

EPILOGUE

As we approach the end of Whispers of the Inner Mind, it is clear that the journey is not about reaching a destination but rather about uncovering layers of insight and experience within oneself. Each poem has served as a chapter in this unfolding story of the self—a story that does not end with the final page but instead opens into a renewed, awakened perspective of life.

In "Realms of Astral Planes," we conclude with a reminder of the boundlessness of inner exploration. This piece invites us to consider the mind as an endless landscape where mysteries reside beyond our conscious grasp. As readers, we are left with the idea that self-discovery is not a finite quest but a continual process of opening, evolving, and transcending what we know of ourselves.

Reflecting, each poem in this collection represents a facet of the human condition. Pieces like "Echoes of Lost Heritage" remind us of our roots, cultural memories, and histories that shape our sense of belonging. Others, like "Mirrors of Positivity and Growth," challenge us to face our self-reflections to see how we might grow by cultivating positivity within. The cumulative effect is a tapestry woven from diverse threads of self-awareness, inviting us to reflect on the interconnectedness of all things—past, present, and future.

Whispers of the Inner Mind is more than a collection of poems; it is a toolkit for personal growth, a sanctuary of introspection, and a source of quiet empowerment. In reading, one finds that each poem is a guide, offering insight and perspective to take beyond the page and into daily life. In times of difficulty or doubt, readers may return to poems like "Faith," "The Weight of Thoughts," and "Embracing Optimism" to find solace, encouragement, and clarity.

The underlying message is clear: within each of us lies an infinite capacity for transformation and growth. Though marked by challenges, life's journey is also filled with opportunities to discover inner resilience and deeper understanding. As you close this book, consider the inner landscape you have explored—the mountains of self-doubt you have crossed, the valleys of acceptance you have rested in, and the rivers of inspiration you have followed. The journey may be personal, but its themes are universal, and each reflection and revelation adds to the collective story of human experience.

The epilogue, like the collection itself, is an invitation. It invites readers to take what they have gained in these pages and let it influence their lives. Let the insights you have gathered guide your interactions, choices, and relationship with yourself. Each whisper of wisdom found here is not an end but a beginning—a seed that can grow, flourish, and manifest in all areas of life.

As you close Whispers of the Inner Mind, know that the journey inward is one of boundless potential. The echoes of these poems remain, guiding, comforting, and challenging you to listen to the quiet voice within. May this collection serve as a lasting reminder of the beauty and strength that lie at the core of the self, and may it inspire you to continue the journey of self-discovery with courage, compassion, and an open heart.

ABOUT THE AUTHOR

Click on Photo to Access Author Page

Mr. SWAMINATHAN MURALI

A doyen with a prosperous 33 years of experience in the oil field. Being a Science talent scholar, he has done his M.Sc. (Hons) in Chemistry and M.Sc. (Hons) in Biological Sciences from the prestigious Birla Institute of Technology & Science, BITS PILANI, an MBA with specialisation in Operations Research, Oracle Certified Data Base Manager, Black Belt in Six Sigma and a PMP certified Professional of PMP-USA. On joining the prestigious Maharatna E & P company, he rose to the Head of Material Management level with a score of officers and staff under his guidance and mentorship until his superannuation.

Contact Author - smuralis2000@gmail.com

YOUR VALUABLE REVIEW

A Humble Request

Could you please leave a review on the book? One last time! I'd love it if you could leave a review about the book. Reviews may not matter to big-name authors, but they're a tremendous help for authors like me, who don't have much following. They help me grow my readership by encouraging folks to take a chance on my books. To put it straight– reviews are the lifeblood of any author. Please leave your feedback on the seller's website book review page.

It will take less than a minute of yours, but it will tremendously help me reach out to more people, so please leave your review. Thank you for supporting my work, and I'd love to see your book review.

OTHER BOOKS FROM THE AUTHOR

Click on Image to Access Book

THE ART OF WAKING UP TO HAPPINESS

Awakening Happiness and Unveiling The Path to Blissful Success, Embracing Joy, And Navigating Life's Purposeful Journey

http://tinyurl.com/mpefa4w2

MUSINGS

A Melange of Poetic Reflections, Emotions, And Philosophical Thoughts of Inner Awakening

http://tinyurl.com/2p8nnvvx

RHYTHM OF LIFE

A Poetic Ode on Philosophical Thoughts, Psychological Behaviour, Emotions In Tranquility and Inner Awakening

http://tinyurl.com/hej77hbw

OTHER BOOKS FROM THE AUTHOR

Click on Image to Access Book

SUNRISE OF THE SOUL

Echoes of the Ethereal Heart, Awakening the Symphony of Sentience, Embracing the Euphony of Inner Light, Awakening Uncharted Realms

https://tinyurl.com/529hzakb

FUNDAMENTALS OF REALITY

Bridging Science and Philosophy: Delving into Quantum Realms, Cosmic Mysteries and the Time-Space Continuum for Transformative

https://tinyurl.com/mry7fxa4

REALMS OF ASTRAL PLANES

Exploring the Mystical Realms of Astral Planes: Unveiling Hidden Dimensions, Awakening Consciousness, and Embracing Cosmic Wisdom. Space. -COSMOS AND ASTRAL PLANES Book 2

https://tinyurl.com/mhkev839

OTHER BOOKS FROM THE AUTHOR

Click on Image to Access Book

THE ART OF WAKING UP TO HAPPINESS VOL 2

The art of Radiant Living, Emotional Resilience, Renewed Energy, and the Transformative Power of Positivity

https://tinyurl.com/mr65uxna

THE MIND-REALITY CONNECTION

Unlock the Potential for Personal Growth, Attain Clarity In Shaping Destiny, And Harnessing
The Power Of Mind To Transform Life.
(EMOTIONS IN TRANQUILITY Book 3)

https://tinyurl.com/5d5v33x6

EMOTIONAL ALCHEMY

Master Your Feelings: Cultivate Mindfulness, Strengthen Empathy, and Foster Growth for Lifelong Emotional Well-Being
(EMOTIONS IN TRANQUILITY Book-4)

https://tinyurl.com/yuxb6ud8

OTHER BOOKS FROM THE AUTHOR

Click on Image to Access Book

INTERPERSONAL UNDERCURRENTS

Empathy, and Psychosomatic Factors of the Heart-Mind combine for Effective Interpersonal Relations

https://tinyurl.com/3vyxd9te

THE COGNITIVE EMOTIONAL INTELLIGENCE

Exploring impacts of Emotional Intelligence in our lives, Evaluation of EI, Improving Self-awareness with Compassion ... Empathy. (EMOTIONS IN TRANQUILITY Book 1)

https://tinyurl.com/37sent9k

SUNRISE SERENITY

Cultivate Inner Peace and Positivity in Daily Life Embrace Life's Challenges with Grace: Nurture a Life of Purpose and Intention for ... ART OF WAKING UP TO HAPPINESS -1 Book 3)

https://tinyurl.com/y4x9p29p

OTHER BOOKS FROM THE AUTHOR

Click on Image to Access Book

HONING TEAM-BUILDING SKILLS FROM NATURE

Art of building Strong Cohesive, Collaborative Teams; Understanding importance of Emotional Intelligence in Leadership

https://tinyurl.com/mr2f7j9f

EMOTIONAL LIBERATION
Launching Soon

The Importance Of Self-compassion & Self-care, The Challenges Of Overcoming Resistance, & The Necessity Of Resilience In The Face Of Setbacks.

Coming Soon

ACKNOWLEDGEMENT

This entire compilation would not have taken this shape without the soul-inspiring encouragement from Mr. Ranjit Jose, (ranjitjos@gmail,com)who was instrumental in the beautiful cover and interior design and a mentor in the finer aspects of the intricacies of the layout and design.

I will only succeed in my duty if I acknowledge the understanding and cooperation of my wife, Latha, for her encouragement.

Last, I thank my son and daughter for their support and my two lovely grandchildren, who kept my attention while I scribbled this book.

COPYRIGHT

Copyright©2024SwaminathanMurali

All rights reserved. No part of this publication may be reproduced or transmitted in any form or by any means, mechanical or electronic, including photocopying or recording, by any information storage and retrieval system, or by email or any other means whatsoever without permission in writing from the author. No part of this book may be reproduced in any form without permission in writing from the author.

For any queries, please feel free to contact me at:

smuralis2000@gmail.com

Printed in Dunstable, United Kingdom